The Lion of Basantar

Ankit Tripathi

BookLeaf Publishing

India | USA | UK

Presentation by *BookLeaf Publishing*

Web: www.bookleafpub.com

E-mail: info@bookleafpub.com

ISBN: 9789363303515

First edition 2024

I dedicate this attempt to my beloved Vaani

ACKNOWLEDGEMENT

I would like to thank, especially, my student Rudransh Sharma who contributed to the completion of this book. Without his much-needed assistance, I wouldn't be writing this.

The Lion of Basantar

My son, Arun;
No! Second lieutenant Arun
Is not just my son,
He is a big gun—
The gun the boom
Of which deafened
The enemy,
Blew to pieces mercilessly
his nefarious designs
like some dirty scum.
The enemy—dumb
Enough to lay claim on
Our sacred land
Thinking it to be
a low-hanging fruit plum—
was given a nice lesson
in the war-craft by my son,
Second Lieutenant Arun.

Taking forward the tradition
Of our family and country,
My son, who shall be
A guiding star—the sun—
For so many after him,
Joined the Indian Army
On June, The third,
Nineteen sixty-seven.
It was during his YOC—
He was in Ahmednagar when
He was stunned
By an order to hurry
Back to his regiment,
Seventeenth battalion
The Poona horse,
And pick up his gun
And point it at the enemy
In the frontier western.

These orders to scurry
Might have brought misery
Or raised consternation
In the heart of the ordinary;
However, he was military—
A notch above everyone.
He lived to see action—
Action to him was an occasion—
Auspicious and August—-
a sum
Of games and fun

Which required courage
More than a tonne,
Which demanded both—
Not just one—
Splendor and bravery fearsome!

The moment had sounded
The bugle,
The battle had come knocking
At the doors—
Shaking our bed
and the dinner table.

The moment that would horrify
Even the bravest of the men,
The moment only gods themselves
Could look into the eye,
The moment that forced
The Lion—my son—out of his den,
The Lion—whose meager roar
Would echo as an inspiring lore
Across the generations that went by
And the ones that are
Yet to knock at the door.

My son—such a lion he was!
A lion with fine canines
Of courage
And cleaving claws,
A lion who never weighed what wage
He would get in return

Or how much would be the spillage
In the bloody mission.
He left these calculations
To those who planned their days,
Weeks and months in assumptions.
He lived from moment to moment,
No questions or lament.

I might as well compare my son,
Arun, no! Second Lieutenant Arun
To a soaring falcon
Who had known
No other way to deal with the adversary
Than to use his talons.

My soaring falcon, Arun,
Soon transformed into
A swooping falcon
Heading off Towards his prey
Or whoever is in the way
Very near or far away
to take him in his stormy sway.

Before leaving for the hunt,
He stole a little life
To spend with us,
To lend us those last laughs
Before the imminent strife
That would befall us.

Carting along his Java bike

I had gifted him, he reached us,
Knocked at the door,
His mother opened it
first a chink,
Then more, and more.
In his black armoured corps
Dungarees stood he,
Looking more than ever
Ready to fly and soar.

My wife, his mother,
Showered his son
In her maternal love—
No ordinary emotion,
It was eternal love.
The eternal love
That exhorted her son,
With no trace of sorrow,
To fight tooth and nail,
To tail
The enemy right into his burrow.

She, her mother, asked Arun
To leave a blazing trail behind him
That would be trodden
By many more to come
After him.

Soon, Arun, No!
Second Lieutenant Arun
Boarded his train to Jammu

And his mother, Mammu,
And all of us alike,
Glued ourselves to Radio Ceylon
Which had been reporting all along
In vivid detail
Who put up a stout fight
And who fell over frail
In the battle tale—
The tale of valor and might.
Sometimes the strength
Of the signal was five,
Other times it would
Take a nosedive.

Days scurried past, I remember
And it was 16, December,
The year was 1971.
Radio Ceylon reported
A massive tank battle
At Shakargarh.
Our hearts—
They stopped beating
Lest they miss out on
Any details coded
In the signals
That were, at times, wheezing.
Arun's regiment, 17 Poona Horse,
Was posted in this very sector,
We sat, with our fingers
Twisted into a cross,
Thinking,

"Did our son, Arun,
fight?
If yes, how did he fare?
Did the enemy dare
To stop his march,
The show of his might?
Our son must have unleashed
An avalanche of shells
To slay
The enemy notorious,,
He must have paved the way
For the march victorious
Of the Indian Military glorious."

Next morning,
The Prime minister announced,
And with that our hearts bounced,
The ceasefire,
And the battle was over
With all its consequences dire.
However, we were
Happy
As it signaled the homecoming
Of the battle-hardened and burnished
Officer, Second Lt. Arun Khetrpal!

His room was cleaned up,
His bike was sheened up,
And his other stuff was
Kept where he preferred
It the most;

We wanted to host
A grand feast
On this, once in a lifetime, return
Of our son, Arun.

December 19, 1971
The doorbell cried
At which I tried
To brush off the premonitions
Cropping up every now
And every then.
Meanwhile, My wife,
Arun's mother opened the doors
First a chink,
My worst fears accumulated
On the brink
Of my eyes,
The sighs got heavy and fast,
I sat there aghast
Waiting to overhear
What I had already been hearing
Within—no surprise!
So she opened the doors,
First a chink and then more,
And more,
There stood at the door
Opened wide,
The news of his demise.
No! The term is "martyrdom."
The news of his martyrdom.

The Immortals of Rashtriya Rifles

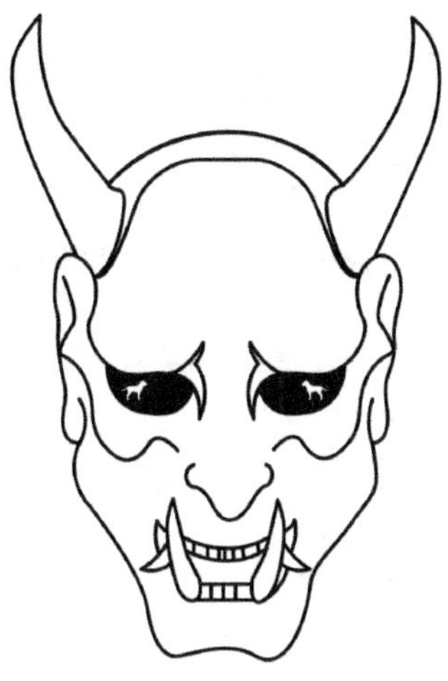

We were in our mess in our nightly dress
waiting for the platter of BADA-KHANA to
arrive.
BADA KHANA?
Yes! This is how we throw a party
In the INDIAN FAUJI TRADITIONS.
BADA KHANA!
It, indeed, was going to be a big meal
to celebrate the "big success" we hunted
in our last operation—no casualties,
no injuries.
A clean operation.
Every operation we plan is unique in itself
and every operation we plan is

always a notch above.

Seventy plus hours
but the operation actually
raised the bars
of our precision and skill
with which we fire and kill.

Everyone—my jawans, JCOs and other officers
were
having a gala time having tasted
life in its best flavour.
Laughing and chatting,
Singing and dancing,
Clapping and tapping
To celebrate the laps of life
lapping within.

Celebrate the laps of life?
Yes! Something that every one of you should do
But you don't.
Because you take these repetitive pulses
That come and go like waves on shores,
for granted.
You don't seem to appreciate that
Every living moment
Is death delayed.

I think this is the difference between a living man
and a dead.
A paradox, as it may appear, but a living man

is constantly thankful for this extra moment
Whereas a dead one is oblivious of the life force
expressing itself through him.

As I contemplated all this,
I closely scanned through every smile
and found everything very human
Yet very superhuman—EVERY MAN AN
EMPEROR!

How these humans transform themselves into lions
While taking those fearless steps alongside me
In the operations.
They march like immortals.

THE IMMORTALS!

This is what our regimental motto is.

"RING RING RING RING"

This was our Battalion Threat signal
and required us all in five to six minutes to
Brief, to plan, to strategize, to gear up
and to mount.

The immortals of my company scrambled
and in no time we rolled out of our gate
on which it was painted,
"YOU WILL CERTAINLY SEE ACTION,
AND YOU WILL SEE IT TODAY ITSELF"

Sitting in the MPV, I again glimpsed through each
face
trying to trace a line of doubt or fear or inhibition.
I could find none.
They all were intense in their gaze,
They all had their finger on the trigger
of their AKs.

Their eyes were blazing,
faces were relaxed.
It was no new task,
It was their routine gaming.

Seek the target and destroy it.

When these men come out of their gates,
They don't go back without their kill.

Our ride came to a jerky halt,
Gates opened
And everyone of us instinctively spilled around
Laying a cordon, almost with a predisposition
taking our respective position.

Announcement was made to stay indoors
For the common civilian
And to come out of doors, for the enemy,
With his hands thrown up in the air.

He didn't heed our warnings.

The house we cordoned up
Turned into hell fire
With all its windows spewing
Flashes of automatic gunfire.

We returned bullet to bullet,
Round to round simultaneously
Closing in organically on the target
Which was a typical Kashmiri home—
The ground floor, then the first floor,
Next the attic on the top
With a chimney billowing out
Smoke into the azure.

As I was trying to ascertain
The number of terrorists hiding inside
By observing the pattern
And the frequency of the fire,
The bushes behind me were snapped off
In a flash
And the grass beneath was dug out and trash
Flung into my face
In a matter of a moment.

Instinctively, I brought myself completely
In line with the tree-trunk.
It was an entire AK magazine
that was being emptied at my position.
The sturdy tree took it upon itself
To face the flames and save me up

for some other time.

This heavy barrage of bullets
Intended to take me out
Incensed up my guys
Who went all guns blazing
In the direction of the menacing fire.

At this moment, they all appeared like
great sages-all their senses
aligned in one line.

If it did not involve blood-shed and death
and destruction, it would make a fantastic
Light and sound spectacle with red-hot barrels
blowing out constant bright flashes
complemented with deafening booms.

Soon our collective consciousness realized
That the house, for sometime, had been silent,
No more gunfire had been coming from it.
It was no more violent.

Just to be double-sure,
Our party fired a few more shots only
to be returned by their own echo.
"Have we neutralized the threat
Or are they deceiving us?"

The hit team closed in onto the house,
Broke into it and ransacked it

For any possible menace.

There was no one else left—
Only the three disfigured bodies
Lying in a smear of gore, life-bereft.

We had almost summed up
When the indistinct murmur of our men
was interrupted by a loud bang of AK!

Sepoy Tejinder Singh—A Khalsa—
had succeeded in sniffing out
the last threat hiding in the chimney.
He came under burst fire from a rat
Holed up into the funnel; however, he managed
To steer clear of it.

In the final bid to escape
The might of The Rashtriya Rifles,
The terrorist climbed further up the chimney,
Sneaked out of the upper end and
Took a leap of death
Onto the ground in the compound.

His landing was botched up
by a hammock hung across the lawn.
Its ropes completely rotated him mid-air
leading to his crashing.
In spite of the fact
That his head took the whole impact,
His instincts propelled

Him to spray bullets at anyone
He could lay his eyes on.

The operation had to reach its culmination
so we, THE IMMORTALS, took him down
instantly before any further damage
Could be done to anyone.

Another feast awaited us
back at our den.

The Revenge of General Maximus

Most emperors that I, thus far, witnessed,
My king appeared to be
the most god-fearing
and the most justice-loving.

He ruled not only by brute force
But also by a band of ideals and Maxims—
Maxims that apply everywhere, at all times.
I assumed his reign would be a part of folklore.

Of all his lieutenants and generals and advisors
That assisted and protected and tendered advice,
I, he said, was the most trusted of all the
supervisors.

So, who am I?

I was the shield of both, the emperor
and the empire,
I stood guard at the front to keep the fire
burning in the hearths of the Roman Empire,

The symphony emerging from the lyre
of my civilized society is what I lived
to preserve and serve with great fervor.

The first line of defense of the empire
and
the last argument of the emperor
is what the emperor declared me to be!

My name is General Marcus Nonius "Maximus",
I towered above all the military officials
of the mighty military of the Roman Empire
Helmed by Marcus Aurelius the Great!

However, his fate
had come a full circle of
Childhood, youth and Old age.
Death is another circle altogether.

He lost his vitality.
The kingship had cost him
His near and dear ones—
Seldom did he come across people
Who bore love and loyalty.

As he was coming to terms with this abrasion,
he lost his hold and say
on the matters of the administration
To his ambitious biological heir—

Commodus—his legit son.

I must clarify that
He was just an heir to the throne,
Not a son to a father.
His father, the emperor, did not see him
In good light.
Being his father,
He was well aware
Of his interests and inclinations
That would be detrimental to the
Longevity of the empire.

The emperor was convinced
That Commodus was not
An able ruler, he knew naught
About the empire and the people.
He lacked the courage and the spirit
Of a king.
Battles scared him,
Women allured him
Before anything else—
No virtue did he possess
To reign the empire in;
Only sin
For as deep as the emperor
Could see through his actions.

One evening the Emperor sent for me

to discuss the matters of the state and
Of passing on of the baton thereof.
I appeared before him as a general;
however, he treated me as a son-
as an heir to the throne.
He assumed I could steer the fate
Of Rome
In the right direction
And mold it to get the right form.

This late evening meeting set the
furnace of rumors across the empire
ablaze.
There were questions raised
On my intentions and the devotion
of the old emperor for his powerful general
Became a matter of contention.
Rumors led to more rumors
Which were largely right.
The king indeed wanted me to
assume the power superseding
his son—Commodus.

Giving the series of events a new swing,
Commodus got the emperor murdered
Under the cloak of darkness and
Had me arrested and escorted
To a remote location to be executed.
At the same time, to get rid of any other threat

Springing from my death,
he also dispatched his assassins
To my village to ravage my beautiful wife
And murder my brave, five-year-old son.

I managed to dodge the blade
Being a hardened warrior,
My family could not, however.
They were just farmers, not warriors,
Working with a shovel and spade.

The little bubble of my family was brutally
burst.
My wife was tortured before she was
crucified alive and set afire.
My son could not be tortured;
He left at the first blow itself on his head.

The skirmish with the assassins
Left a deep wound in my left, lower back.
It was an easy passage for blood to flow out
And worms to dig in.
In spite of the weakening perception,
I rode to my village presageful
Of the worst possible situation.

The murderous act had already been executed.
I got to my wife, who had been ravaged

And burnt and killed and nailed to a wooden pier
Up higher than the highest tree.
Then I stumbled upon the other charred but
smaller body—
That of my son's.
It felt as if all the struggle
And any further trouble is for nothing now
and
I lay motionless at the jamb of life and after-life
Trying to weigh in the consequences
Of staying here or crossing over.

In a near-dead condition, I was carried away
by a few nomadic passers-by.
They were slaves themselves and turned me
into one.
I now reflect back on that time and
draw an important lesson—
there is no watertight criterion
about judging loyalty and perfidy—
Even dark-skinned slaves can be loyal
friends.
On the other hand, blue blood
Can be sans
Loyalty and integrity.

Oblivious of the wounds within,
Those African slaves took good care of me
To rid me of the scars on my head and back.

Months went by and I regained my strength
And made a few friends among those victims of
slavery.
With revived strength and new friends came
determination—
Determination to settle scores with the
perpetrators of
The atrocity.

Something kept goading me—
it kept whispering in my ear,
"VENGEANCE, VENGEANCE,
VENGEANCE!
You must stay to wreak vengeance
Upon Commodus, the new evil king."

The desire within and the supernatural
turn of events without brought me
Back to where I started from—
Rome.

My muscle memory as a warrior
Rose me above the crowd of slaves,
The slaves began counting my name in Braves.
My fame as a great, fearless fighter soon
Traveled across the lands of deserts.
Slave masters thronged to buy me for the highest
Price they could afford.

I, as a fighter, changed hands until I was bought
By the one who would take me to Rome to make
A gladiator out of me to be pitted against the
Deadliest of opponents ranging from Lions and
Tigers to beastly giants.

I always managed to give death a miss.
No matter who stood in my way, I crushed
him and stood victorious amidst
the cheering crowd of the Colosseum.

My fame spanned, though under a different
name and identity—
Not just across the common alley
Of the city,
but it sent shockwaves through
The royal quarters of the Roman nobility.

The unsettled emperor, one day,
Came to be a witness to the smooth
Flicks of "THE GLADIATOR" in the arena.
The announcements were made
And the arena had a different appearance
In the honor of the emperor.

After the event was over
With "THE GLADIATOR"
declared the victor,
He descended from his high seat

And landed into the arena
To felicitate me, THE GLADIATOR,
For my skill and prowess.

Landing there, he asked me for my name
And I did not utter a word,
He insisted again on
Knowing who I was,
Yet I did not utter a word.

At last he ordered me to take off
My mask!

The mask was detached
And the coward lurched
In his shoes.
"I am Marcus Nonius Maximus,
The commander of the armies of the north,
The loyal servant to the true emperor,
Marcus aurelius,
Father to a murdered son,
Husband to a murdered wife
And I will have my revenge
In this life or the next!"

He couldn't have put me to death
For the colosseum was echoing
With the chants of my new name
And identity—the gladiator!

The coward returned to his palace
With a twisted countenance.

He planned to
Immediately put me to death
In the dark dungeons of the fortress.
However he was under duress
From the political advisors that kept him
From making such a move,
For it would have turned
the common man
Against the Emperor—
"A blunder! A blunder it would be,
My lord!" they snarled.

So, after much deliberation, he decided
To face me in the Colosseum
To exemplify his bravery by killing
"The invincible general."
It required courage and skill; something
He did not acquire in his profligate life.

 So his flagitious self came up
with a flagitious trick to kill two birds
with one stone—
To have me injured the night before the duel,
To have my spirits battered.

The trick was to inflict a wound just deep
enough
for the blood to trickle out drop by drop
Away from the common man's eyes.
He assumed it would drain all my vigor
Leaving me unable to dodge his sword—
My thighs would tremble,
Arms would not be able to grip the hilt
And
He would "fight" and kill "the invincible
gladiator"
The next morning in front of
The entire Roman folk to prove his
puissance.

'Twas the night before the encounter with evil.
The coward must have been very worried for
I was not one of those meek, alluring women
He toyed with,
I was the General,
So he, himself, marched up to me
Under the guise of darkness.
I was chained and he was free.
For a while, he ranted on about many things,
About how his father, to him, had been unfair,
How, he thought, I would serve him
With all my flair,
Then, just before leaving, he clenched me
In his arms—

I felt a sharp pain penetrating
Somewhere deep inside my abdomen.
He stabbed me and left me alone
for the entire night to bleed.

He must have thought that the
dripping blood
would drip the strength out of
my limbs
Leaving me lamblike
Which it did to an extent
Which was not enough
To render me inoperative.

The sun rose pretty late that morning,
For each second took away a drop
And each drop took away an ounce
Of strength and light from my eyes
which were going hazy.

The gongs echoed, finally;
I was brought out into the arena.
This was going to be the last battle
of my life with the shadow of evil
on earth.

With a will to win him over
And gift his death
To my wife and child, I mustered

The remaining strength, clustered it
Into a double-edged sword
And struck him so hard that
The entire stadium fell silent
with the falling of the lifeless
emperor.

I could hear no noise, I could feel no pain,
I could see no blood or mud.
Just immense peace, just a long silence
After a long life scattered with plenty
Episodes of violence.

The story of Ibex

The Rockies have always been merciful
to us, to give these towering giants their dues,
Since the beginning of their life.

My ancestors, their ancestors and theirs—
Everyone found a place to place themselves
slouchily
With a refuge on his head to dodge
the fiery force of fierce elements.

You're probably wondering
what this faceless voice is!
This is I, The Ibex, who am echoing
within these rocky Juggernauts.

Your wonder still seems to be continuing
about my name, The Ibex.

Well, I am sort of a goat
tweaked about by the creator
to make me stout enough
to survive the mountains.

I have been hand-made
to rip through the rigors
of the rigorous Rockies.

Okay, so here on I begin
to speak for my benign
individual self—
In the lines above,
I spoke for our entire benign race.

Not far from here
In the upper reaches of Northern Alberta
There is a restive peak
with a remote cave
by the banks of the Bigoray river.

In the cozy cave,
I, along with my other siblings,
was born to my fleecy, formidable mother.
My father was standing guard
to watch out for any Intruder
In the face of a bald eagle
out of the blue,
or a cougar

trying to rip through our safe shelter and
unsafe lives.

Soon, I grew up to stand firm
on all fours
and not be a wobbly specimen
ready to be served at somebody's supper.
My phantom father always made sure
that my mushy mother
and I, along with my other siblings,
Felt safe enough to spend quality time
among ourselves.

We hopped, we chased, we leapt, we played,
Mumma taught us many a time
to bleat in sync and rhyme.
She inculcated those precious survival tactics,
honed our instincts
to keep ourselves biologically on.

We munched on the soft, juicy grass the whole
day
And learnt to avoid lurching on the steep slopes
of the rugged Rockies.

Earlier, at times I felt the sharp slopes to be
cursed,
For they bore witness to the worst
that could befall anyone.

These rocks and boulders and heaps of mud
closed in on all my siblings, my mother, my
father and a few others.

However, now as the only living member
of our loving family
I don't feel the same anymore.
These sky-scraping hills are, in fact, blessed
nurturing all of us—
the loving and the warring alike—
offering all of us an equal gamble
to prove our prowess.

Those of us who prove pre-emptive,
go on
and those who don't,
Perish.

A five-year-old and his military dad

After having stayed together for two years
On his first-ever peace posting,
We had to split into two;
Mumma, Shivam—my younger brother—
and I had to stay back in Meerut
and Dad had to leave for Jammu and Kashmir,
Somewhere along the Line of Control.

It was going to be the first time
when we would be living
all by ourselves in a place
that did not give solace
like our native village.

I know one might think two odd years

should be enough to build rapport
with a new place and strange people.
To a great extent, this line of thought
is logical;
however, it is not as practical
for a newly married young woman
straight out of a remote Indian village
as for the readers carrying smartphones
in their palms and laptops on their laps.
Of course, Army takes care of most things
of a family of a personnel serving
in the field areas;
Still, it can't solve a few odd issues
like a fearful wife missing her husband
and children growing up in constant fear
of their father's dead body arriving
in a tri-colored coffin
any day at their doorstep.

Those were not unfounded, baseless
fears resulting out of overthinking.
It was real! Coffins had arrived in the past
in our neighborhood and those anecdotes kept
the fears alive in our fragile hearts and
strong minds.

Plus, the first times are mostly bewildering
for most ordinary people.
We were no exception—it was our first time

and we were ordinary.

I don't know what must have gone on
between my military mom and military dad,
but I can tell you, it was pathetic for a child
of five to ignore the elephant in the room.

I kept asking my mom if the transfer orders
could be canceled,
if something could be tweaked with
in order to keep my dad from going
to the place of origin of the most
horrible stories of valor and sacrifice.

I did not want my father to be a hero
of those valorous chronicles
to be remembered for generations
to arrive; I, only, wanted him
to be an ordinary father.
A father who is there for his children
every day to play, to study, to scold.

My repeated inquiries, however, served
no purpose.
The day drew near and one morning
at 5 o'clock, even though it was
pitch dark, I, a kid of five,
was woken up
by a lot of noise.

What I saw brought my heart
almost into my mouth.
Dad was all decked up in his
combat uniform with his cap on.
At his side was his bedroll and other
military stuff. There was that peculiar
smell of "Brasso" and Cherry shoe polish
filling the entire house.
As I keenly observed the camouflaged
patterns on his uniform, my ears were
alarmed by the horn of a gypsy waiting
out to take him away.

Two Jawans soon marched in,
saluted him, "JAI HIND, SAAAB,"
in their Tamilian accent, lifted his
luggage and marched out carrying it
on their shoulders.

With their marching out, marched out
the last hope.
Dad hopped onto the gypsy
drove away leaving behind
the familiar smell of Brasso
and Cherry Shoe polish mixed up with
the Fumes of petrol.

Where is Rajkaran?

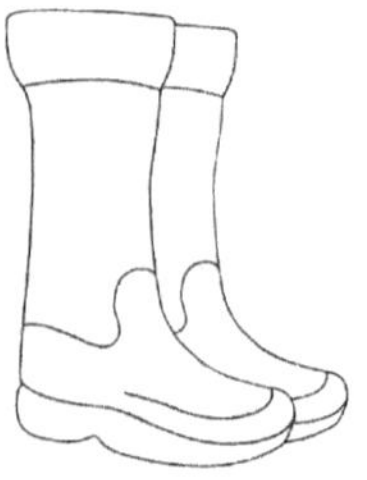

His name was Rajkaran—a student at a private
college
at Prayagraj.
A very affable and gentle being—
no one had ever seen
Him in any other state than that of happiness.
Full of life and full of fervor of friendliness.
Even though he came from a deprived family,
He didn't let that melancholy
Hinder his disarming smile.
While all the teachers adored him for his
dedication towards
His studies, Arun sir, his Sanskrit teacher,
particularly
Showered him with a fatherly affection.

Arun sir was a god-gifted teacher—
A creature who could sniff out
The students who really had a penchant for
Making it big in studies.
He, often, discussed Rajkaran's scholarly

Behavior with his newly-wed wife.
Kind-hearted as his wife was,
she agreed to her husband's proposal
To support him in his literary journey
With both money and morale.

Rajkaran's yearning for learning
And Arun sir's obsession with teaching
Had no parallel in the entire college.
It could have been a fruitful combination
If only Rajkaran had not been lethally gullible.

Just as Arun sir noticed his strength
and decided to take it upon himself
to mentor him,
Rajesh—another student of his class—
noticed his naivety and settled down to exploit it
to his best.
Rajesh came from a wealthy business family.
He was basking in the money flowing in from
various
Liquor outlets and bars that his father owned.
Ever since he opened his eyes to the world,
And gained a sense of life,
He felt money rushing into his pockets without
making any effort.
It was enough to make him spendthrift and
careless towards studies.

He couldn't really think of any reason to tilt his
head down into books.
This neglect, more often than not, drew the irk
of the teachers,
Especially Arun sir.
So regular the punishments meted out to him
had become
that he grew increasingly thick-skinned.
Not just thick-skinned but rebellious as well!

One evening when Arun sir was out in the
market
Hoarding household items, he caught sight of
Rajkaran
Sipping tea alongside Rajesh at a rundown tea
stall.
"Rajkaran with Rajesh," he mumbled to himself.
Right there, he peeped far into future and
witnessed
His favorite student getting lost in the darkness
of glamor
Which scared him more than ever. "It is a
possibility staring
Straight into the poor boy's face," he murmured
and left the
Place to itself.
The marketplace was left to itself, not Rajkaran.
Next day he sent for him the first thing in the
morning.

As soon as he stepped into his office,
Arun sir read him the riot act
For hanging out with"a rogue of a chap!"
Realizing the intensity of his upbraiding,
He switched to his brotherly mode,
And placed his palm on his shoulder.
Placing his sincere palm on Rajkaran's shoulder,
He advised him against keeping himself
In such a ruinous company.
Arun sir's advice, however, could not have as
great an effect
As Rajesh's enticement for a "grand and
luxurious life" could.

A week went by and Rajesh told him about this
new liquor factory
That his maternal uncle had set up
Just 70 km from there in a languid village,
Phulpur.
He lured him to Come and see for himself
How huge the plant is and then decide if
He could resist working in such a majestic
setting.
Noticing the changes on Rajkaran's innocent
countenance,
And the dreams of getting rich
Coming alive in his eyes,
He further assured him of regular sums of
money

With which
He could put an end to the impoverished state
Of his widowed mother
And three handicapped younger brothers.

To wipe off the last streak of hesitation that still
remained
In Rajkaran's eyes,
Rajesh's claims of assured wealth and affluence
Got taller and grander leaving no room
For Rajkaran's mind to deal with it realistically.
He readily agreed to go along with him
To the liquor factory at Phulpur.
Leaving the hostel and venturing as far as 70 km
was not a piece of cake
For a villager like him.
It demanded so many questions to be answered.
So many inquiries had to be dealt with.

To avoid all the trouble
They both decided to sneak out after evening tea
without telling anything to anybody.

Evading the garrulous guards and the slack,
barbed wires,
They reached the bus stand and boarded
A bus to Phulpur at 6 in the evening.
After lodging people even in the crevices

Of the dilapidated bus, the driver rolled the bus
out.
One hour into the journey, the conductor fought
through
Every person—sitting and standing—
To reach these two boys sitting at the end.
He asked them to pay for the ticket.
Rajesh slid his hand into the pocket immediately
And pulled out his wallet, fetched a five-rupee
note and
Handed it to the conductor.
Next, the conductor asked Rajkaran for his five
rupees.
This was a moment of fatal realization.
He did not even have a twenty-five paisa Coin.
Before he could say anything,
The changes in the expressions on his pale face
Declared his bankruptcy loud and clear.
The conductor, without wasting a meter more,
Brought the bus to a halt and shunted him out.
The road was silent and still except for the
revving of the bus—
No vehicle around,
No people or their sound.
The bus sped away with its tail lights reddening
his otherwise pale face.
The red on his face faded soon with the fading
of the bus
Into the turn of the winding road.

He stood there in the middle of nowhere nobody
knows for how long.
A few moments or maybe an eternity later he
started to walk in the direction
Of his city only to never reach there.
Nobody ever heard of him again nor did
anybody see him after that day's evening tea.

The first time I saw a train slither

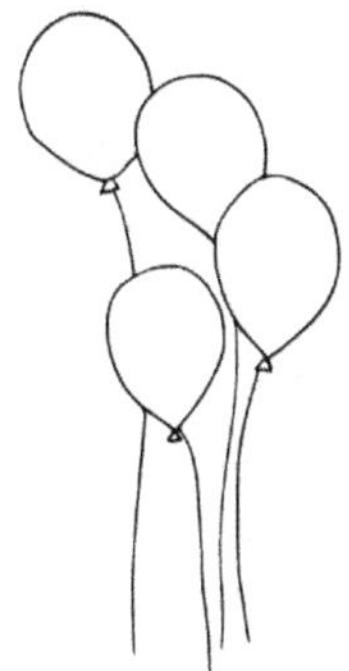

The first time I witnessed a train move
Left me frozen in awe and delusion.

I, a kid of four, was standing on the
overbridge at a railway station.
It was going to be the first-ever
train-journey of my life.

My youthful father
along with his wife—
my mother—
were chatting,
most probably, about
the things around
as I grasped the minute details
of the commotion at the railway station—

The chai-wala selling chai
in his monotonous CHAI-CHAIYYA!,
the coolie in his red outfit commendably
balancing immense weights on his head,
the small beggars lingering about
with their arms stretched out and
palms wide open hoping for alms.

It was just another bustling
marketplace to me until
I noticed one of the
brown-painted houses
with silver roof and unique,
equidistantly carved-out windows
slither like serpents
right under the bridge, we had been
standing on.

"Mumma, Mumma!" I reached out for her
face with my small hands to draw her
attention to this miraculous occurrence.

"Those huts have started sliding!"
I continued with my eyes bulged up
in size.
Mumma could do nothing else but laugh heartily
with her eyes
replete with love,
at my keen, observing eye as also at my

innocent manner of describing things.

It must have, partly, served to bring back
the memories of her childhood as folks
tend to forget what it is like to be a child
in the rat race of growing up into an adult.

Children, in my view, are a kind of anchor
for adults to stay rooted to the child within;
however, unfortunately, far from staying
anchored to their child within, they
get hell-bent upon robbing their children
of their light-heartedness.

"Those are not huts.
That is a moving train," she explained
affectionately, tapping on my cheeks.

Make your child your teacher

A child has his mind
where his eyes are,
unlike grown-ups
who have to remind
themselves to bar
their mind from shuffling
between past and future—
completely missing out
on the present.

It is the grown-ups
who need a tutor
to learn to be cheerful—
instead they keep teaching
children to be "grave" as they age.

A child is cheerful within
notwithstanding the constraints
limiting the prospects of grinning.
So,
instead of trying and impressing

your laborious adulthood
on your children,
it'd do you much good
if you imbibed their chuckling
childhood.

Have you ever noticed
how you keep
out of humour
for
days, months, years
or
in insane cases for the entire
lifetime after
hearing a certain rumour
or
for something unfair
that someone unfair
or
with unfair intentions
did to you a long, long,
A long while ago.

While you keep a grudge
harboured in your heart
that tends to smudge
all your joy and brightness
into one lump
of inexplicable emotion,

it is not so with little,
but more mature (than you at least)
adults.

One moment they get hurt.
They make the entire world
know with their loud shrieks
that they are hurt.
They send out a message curt
either by blurting out
nasty sounding things
or by using their soft, supple limbs.

However, if in the middle of this
mire of tears and blurry vision
they happen to lay their sparkling eyes
or trembling hands
on something that titillates
their little curiosity,
they open up their arms wide
to embrace
the tear-smeared smile
mopping off the tears
along with the reason
that welled up
those tears.

You keep quoting
great sounding lines

of wisdom
about how even at the loss
of kingdom a certain king
did not lose hope,
About how he gripped
on to the sense
of justice of the providence.

Yet you lost it at the first instance
Of misfortune
Those Pompous Poems
that you knead
and pile up
in your head
to be shot at people
suffering any tragedy perchance do not come to
your rescue

Children are not inherently like this—
Janus-faced.
Their head is not laced
Up with moral quotes and
knowledge-filled books.

They are run not by books
but the touch and guidance
of the creator himself
resting in peace
in their innocence.

Ghost Hamlet to Hamlet

Old Hamlet (ghost) speaks

The poison curdled my blood,
My breath fell short,
My eyes stony did turn, my son!
And, thus, I left you, losing the feud
To that killer venom.

My limbs lost their fire,
My heart lost its pulse,
On my face did spread the pallor dire,
And this is how I lost my earthly attire.

My peace, my ease,
My loved ones
And that ephemeral life on lease—
The pain was unmatched

When everything from me
Was away snatched.

I wriggled left, I wriggled right,
I summoned my every ounce to fight,
But every effort—covert or overt
Was in vain,
And there I lay lifeless, slain.
I exhorted my breath to keep blowing,
But the breathlessness kept growing,
There was no way of knowing,
What or who on the soil of my life
Was death sowing.

My limbs trembled,
My lips mumbled,
My voice wambled,
And, death upon my head dangled.

Soon got over the ordeal,
Death, finally, did itself to me reveal,
There are things that I must, from you, conceal,
Just know how the Providence
On my fate as a body-less being put its
Omnipotent seal.

So now,

All the bodily restraints are gone—

Laughter, sob, frown, and moan
Do not twitch anything in me now,
However, there is only one regret
Through which I still plow.

Hamlet speaks back!

What is it, my lord?
And, and how—how did you,
All of a sudden, die?
They say it was a serpent,
Or was it all a big lie?

They say it was a serpent
That fanged venom into your sturdy frame,
Is it really true or just a false claim?
Was it an enemy who acted out of malevolence?
Or was it a loved one bereft of benevolence?

Oh father! Please open your mouth
And let me know
What in the middle of that broad day
Transpired?
Was it really a snake?
Or the enemy of the state
That to usurp the throne aspired?

Father! My lord!
Nothing about your death feels true,

Every fact, almost every fact
Is shrouded in a darkened hue.

Look at how shamelessly your wife,
I beg your pardon,
Your wife has your memories buried,
Then widowed and now remarried.

The day she went ahead
With that hasty remarriage,
She did lose her child as well
In a tragic miscarriage.

Neither a wife nor a mother
Does she remain,
She has lost that aura, that sheen,
The only identity that she retains yet
Is that of a carnal queen.

Old Hamlet speaks again!

It's Claudius,
Your Uncle,
My brother,
The mole is Claudius—

He emptied the vial of henbane into
My sleeping ear,

To steer of my noble rule clear.
What Goneril and Regan were to lear,
Was Claudius was to me, my son, dear.

Ever since I ascended the throne,
He sought to dethrone me,
And thought he ought to have made it his own
Everything, in his eyes, had been ugly,
So he stood there on one leg like a heron.

Multitudes of attempts at knocking me off
Had he made
Before finally receiving a "well played"
In the shape of my woody corpse
That a day after to rest was laid.

Not just the throne and the state,
He even did play his incestuous games
On my so-called soul mate,
Who to me did seem virtuous
In my living days of yore,
She, in fact, came out to be voluptuous
After I died of that deep wound sore.

She fell for his feigned love,
For faithless gifts,
For his bright prospects
That were wiped clean
After my fall.

His claims of love
That seemed to her grand and tall.

Had she really been virtuous,
She would have resisted that all,
But, her virtue and her loyalty
Withered away,
Just as certain leaves for lack of drizzle
In the autumn do fall.

Anyway,
She might not have held me close to her heart,
But, my young Hamlet,
Her soul to its core does have a warmth
That seeks to preserve you
Like an infant
For whom she will let go
Of everything else right this instant.

So do not speak daggers to her,
Be nice, be gentle, be kind,
Don't lose your mind, be kind.
Also, remember to not tell
These life and death matters to her,
For why must she mourn twice
For a husband who died once.

But it's only your mother
I ask you to be kind to,

Not my wife, not my lover,
And certainly not my promiscuous brother.

As a duty-bound son,
Give Claudius the taste of his own medicine,
He must beg for mercy, he must give out
helpless din,
Leave no stone unturned
To prepare a pyre and set evil afire,
And let me coldly watch it burnt.

Make it, my son, quick,
The dawn is about to break,
You must, as a loyal scion, this vow take,
Do it and do it with your sword in a flick.

Hamlet speaks back for the final time

With all the directions,
Elves, fairies and apparitions
residing therein as my witness!
With this moon,
That yonder sun,
These stars that beam and shine
And twinkle to harness
The universal darkness!
With the ghost of my brutally butchered father
as my witness,
I, The prince of Denmark,

Hamlet, pledges to wreak vengeance
Upon the man who blew out
The guiding light of Denmark,
Leaving it with a future
That appears uncertain and dark.

My Guardian angel

The day you ran into me
was the day the frozen town
of my cold ideas, my bitter notions,
and my decaying contemplations—
came crashing down
like a huge overhang of lifeless
snow and ice.

The hibernating life within was let loose
and it dragged in a gust of fresh air,
stretched its limbs which had been curled close
to forbid anyone from venturing into its lair.

The warmth of your kindness
assured my untouched self
of a hub
where I could strip off all
that had been keeping off
the blooms of fragrance and freshness

from adorning my life bud.

Are you a wizard
or an ancient bard?
What gives you this Savoir fair
to take it upon yourself to guard
the precincts of my existence?

I stand astonished at
how you manage to borrow
every tumult and turbidity
and sadness and sorrow
Sharing the mellifluous notes
of ecstasy and bliss.

Don't you ever get empty
of the divinity?
It's been a while
that you've been emptying
yourself to serve me.

Don't you get done
with the vituperation of this being
with whom you claim to be one?
What is the mystery behind your sheen?

Are you even a human
like all of us, like me?
Or an elf or a fairy

who had descended
only to make a prince of this one?

You appear to me my guardian angel
who has embodied to free me of the tangle
of rudeness, bitterness and soreness.
Your voice sounds like the voice of eternity
Which takes form of a god to bless
alike the mighty and the laity.

Every instance of your presence
feels like the life-essence.
It reverberates the heart within
and then fills it with your
graceful luminescence.

Are you the creator?
Tell me the truth!
Are you the one
Different people call with different names?
Are you the one who, out of mercy and ruth
ordained this union?

Every event looks well-planned,
well-articulated, predestined.
As if you slated it all,
saving me from the worst fall,
to happen well!

As if you slated the tryst,
the hand-holding, the teasing,
the talks, the short walks,
the confession, the expression
of the brewing affection.

As if you staged the embrace,
the kiss, the songs, the grace.
It all looks deliberate on your part
to keep me from you apart
for all these days, weeks
months and years.

As if you sent me through
all the predicaments and fears,
the scary people, the scorching tears
The icy breaths without you
for me to better appreciate
the lordly love of yours!

The way you have handed me your attention—
absolute—no pretension
anywhere in any of your gestures
goes a long way to build my trust
and the belief that love fosters
The godliness inherent in every human.

Finally, I must wind up
by telling you that

You are the best of every story
that—
Cordelia in Lear, the King,
Miranda in the tempest
or
Rapunzel in the tales of Flynn.

Sapience

You know why the earth
doesn't go cold and freeze
and perish after the sun
goes down?

No! Not because it keeps itself
warm with the warmth of stars
strewn across the sky.

It is the assurance;
assurance offered by the sun
that he will return the next day
to rid the earth of its cold scars,
to nourish!

You know why the trees don't
commit suicide when all their
leaves are gone in the fall of
autumn?

No! It is not the freedom from

having to nourish so many offsprings
that keeps them from mourning the loss.

It is the confidence that they bear
in their ability to sprout all the leaves
anew at the onset of spring.

You know why these snakes don't
die of heart attack at the loss of their
warm, deep burrows during the rains?

No! It is not that they don't have a sense
of home.

It is the hope; the hope that,
as long as they have their breath
running,
they
will find another burrow somewhere
to hibernate in winters.

If these so-called inferior (to human)
beings
know how to cope with hardships
what stops us, human beings, from

facing the vicissitudes of life
with fortitude, hope and courage;
in addition to these, we have sapience!

A game of gamble

Yudhishthira speaks—

"I have nothing else left to lose,
My brothers, my crown, my kingdom, my
desires
that I, compulsively, let loose.

What else, what else, Duryodhan,
do you think I must give up
to bring at ease this vicious gamble?

Look at mace—wielding Bheem,
At Arjuna—the bearer of Gandeev
and
His fiery arrows,
At Nakula and his cupid-like sheen,
At Sehdev, at the sight of whose sword
the enemy harrows.

Lying on its belly before you, Duryodhan, is
the majesty of Hastinapur,
Mired in mud, tired and slug
Moaning at the loss of its grandeur.

Our crowns do kiss your unmoving feet,
The throne stands guard to bow and embrace
your fiery heat,
All the pillars and arches stretch higher to meet
your stature high,
Left to me to further fight this battle is nigh."

Replies Duryodhan—

Not so easy! Not so easy
Will I make this game between you and me,
Let me correct myself here quickly,
It is not a game between us.

It is a game between your ego and mine
Your ego which knows no bounds
Your ego which has, in its size and grandeur,
grown elephantine.

Your ego which is fierce,
Your ego which has blazes erupting from its
enlarged maw,
Look at her eyes, the alluring eyes—

The eyes that grip their beholder
As the Jungle-king holds his prey in its claw.

The eyes! The eyes of your ego, Yudhishthira!
Those eyes don't let me catch a wink—
Either at night or in the day
They play
With my esteem around
My self-esteem—the self-esteem of the Scion of
Kuru Vansh
Those finely chiseled eyes,
Those enticing eyes pull me closer to
themselves—
Once, twice, thrice—-
Then they push me away in a blatant display of
mockery
Which, by any standards, is derogatory
To me, my father, my mother and my entire
family.

So, I am not going to make this easy for you,
this game of gamble,
For it will go on until the thighs of your
ravishing ego are torn apart in a jerk
And it comes crashing down to ground not even
fit to wamble.

Bring your ego to the dice board and put all your
stakes on it,

Try your luck at it the last time,
Your luck which, if it takes a turnaround,
might grant you everything you lost, back,
Don't act so slack,
Call upon your wife, next, on the dice,
And throw it away on the board
Along with the hope—
That is bound with victory to elope—
That your despair, as of now, will make way for
your victorious cries."

Yudhishthira agrees to gamble away his wife—
the fire born, Draupadi
To get back what he has lost so far
in this menacing dance of dice
choreographed by their maternal uncle—
the very treacherous Shakuni
And, alas! Loses her; culminating the game,
Setting off a chain of events to defame
The pinnacle of honour and bring shame
to his lineage which has been known to tame
the untamed.

The Kauravas led by Duryodhan inebriated with
victory, guffaw
At the prospects of relishing the woman and the
wealth
that lay at their feet low.

Dushasana brags forward to drag
the grace of Kuru Vansh into the court,
to put a seal of disgrace on the foreheads
of the losers of the day.
With characteristic audacity does he roar,
"Let me have the honour to adorn
my elder brother's triumph
by placing the jewel of Kuru Vansh
in my brother's lap.

The shrieks and moans
of that full-of-herself woman
who is no more than any other queen
Warming the beds of the princes
and the princely men like us."

Saying so he stalks out of the court.
Hurtling towards her chamber,
he pushes aside the men and the objects alike.

Kicking away an old drudge,
smashing apart a vase,
Venting out on her maids his grudge
Pulling down the fine curtains on the way,
He takes everything in his sway.

"Where is that woman who sleeps with five
men?"

he thunders reaching the sill of her room
and enters unhindered.
"Amidst the men by my brother, Duryodhan—
has she been summoned!"

Before the speckless mirror sat speckless
Draupadi.
Visibly enraged and blazed
at this uncontrolled monster at her doorstep.

She orders him out!
Immediately asks her maids to cover her
appropriately,
but before anybody could even blink,
like a volley of arrows,
he pins everyone to the walls and pounces at her.

She swiftly dodges his advances a few times.
However, he, eventually, succeeds
in clenching her long tresses.

While she screams in pain and groans, at the
doom
staring down her eyes—"what audacity!"
she can do nothing in her capacity
to loosen the formidable grip
of those battle-hardened hands.

She resists, she prays,

She again resists, she fails.
She fails to match the speed and the strength
of the beast who was determined
to go to any lengths
to disrobe her.
She staggers and falls over.

He hauls her through the entire
length of the corridors
As a bull lugs a cart in the mire,
Brings her to the doors
of the court in the manner of attire
which was unworthy for a woman
of her sorts.

None could do anything
to prevent this evil
from unfolding further,
Everyone, including the King,
is placed on his seat
like a shoe placed on the anvil
by the cobbler.
They do nothing but repent
being witness to an act so vile.

Nevertheless, there is one man,
The only man, in fact—Krishna—
The king of Dwarka—
Who stands up loud and tall,

Towering above all.
He Rumbles like the dense, ravening clouds
All set to bring the march of scorching summer
To a halt
and deters the atrocious episode
from unfolding further
with his masculine ardour.

A handful of ashes

How must it feel to die,
To leave your feet wobbling,
Your once strong thighs,
Now trembling—sore and trembling,
Your biceps and triceps—
Nothing more than cold tallow,
Your throat gasping,
And, your head,
Your head—numb and hollow?
How must it all feel?
Difficult to swallow?

You claim tall to love your family—
Mother, father, wife and children.
You fear losing them
And your brethren,
Never sparing a thought
About losing yourself

To death!
Death, that is always upon your head
Hovering over.

And one moment!
One moment it grips you tight,
Only then does it dawn upon you—
"It is in vain to give a fight back,
When limbs themselves are getting slack."

Your mother might grip your body
In her mad, motherly embrace,
Still its grip can't be loosened,
Still it can't be won—
The race against time.

Your limbs grow cold,
An under-cold-current of shiver
Takes a stroll across your body.
You feel like hugging her back tight,
But alas! Not enough strength
To fight,
Every attempt to continue
Appears shoddy.
No strength left to cater
To this meagre desire
To hug your mother
To feel alright!
What plight!

The entire life reels before
Your glassy eyes—
Eyes that shed tears of helplessness
In the face of this to-be-separation,
Failure in the face of frustration.

Everyone around shedding tears
On your flimsy to-be-corpse,
Belying all hopes of continuing further.

Your father,
His consoling you,
Standing like a rock,
Holding you,
Holding your head in his strong arms—
His words assuring you of your recovery,
His eyes confronting
Each of the words in his literary inventory.

Nothing withstanding,
You lose the light
Of your eyes—
Weird images float through,
Blurry visions to and fro,
Everything, now, is beyond
The lies and the truths of this world,
The heartbeat has left the heart
And crossed over to the other side

Where there is no sound,
Something still throbs
At the pinnacle of your crown—
The last point of contact between
The life and the body.

Everybody gives it the last shot
Towards bringing your breath back,
By jolting you with electric smack.

But,
You choose to call it a day,
And with that stops the play
Of your life,
The play of failure and success,
Of positions and ambitions,
Of aims and goals.
Everything is reduced to
A handful of ashes.

Whilst I sit in a chair

I say it kills me. You say it cures.
Whilst I sit in a chair, with
nearly a thought to spare,
Barely reaching where I wish to go.

Sometimes I borrow, other times pickpocket
Words to enunciate the void residing within.
Alas! Lexicon falters to bridge the gap betwixt
This parchment and mine bleeding conscience.

Say it is so, say if it ain't so
Dragging these limbs was not what I wished for
Indulging, perhaps over-indulging,
I waste myself whilst all is rotting.

Oh Prometheus, I see thee in anguish,

Suffering for the downtrodden,
Scorching one another with the eternal flame.
How must it feel? Oh how must it feel!

I see one shape come close, close
To my embrace. Hardly it took one look
For me to see that 'twas just my image.
Nothing more, nothing more.

Though that image resembled mine, I sensed
Something faulty inside, it provoked me
To take a closer look, and observe what
Secrets my companion harbored.

Looking down I heard it speak, speak
One thing on and on repeat.
"Come with me. O gentle soul. For
I feel you have settled thine tolls."

Though that voice was sullen and gray
A word of relief it did convey. All it took
Was one last sip of the grog,
And my voice called it back.

Come hither, and touch my embrace.
Pray thee, do so quick, for the clock ain't
stopping.
Come hither, my gentle fate, yearning
Am I for an hour chock full of grace.

Come and fly me to one utopia
Where all is good, and good is great.
Where great men reside, and so
Do bread and wine. Where all are
Awake in eternal sleep.
Where all are renegades and none are sheep.
Where truth is the word and that word, divine.
Where all odds dull, and
Every even shines.

On one fine spring morn

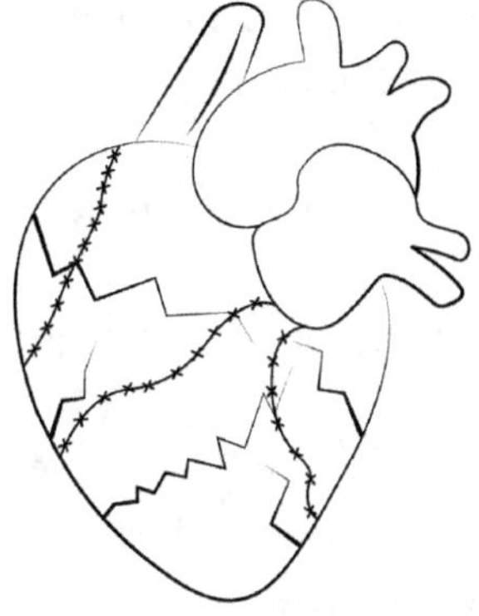

There she stood, in the halo of the morning,
Leaning lightly 'gainst the classroom wall.
Sunlight danced through her locks,
Like a warning, or a siren's call,
That which beckoned me to fall.

Her laughter floated, floated as light as
September's breezy air.
'Twas a melody sung by May's nightingale.
She stood there smiling, effortlessly fair,
In that mundane place.

In that mundane place,
She became my muse amongst the faces.
Around her, time grows cautious, as she
Gently sways in a cinematic frame.
I saw her converse with her friends, in

soft tones of yellow.
Each gesture, each glance of hers, subtly
Proclaimed to me, "Here ends the quest,
For, with her, it all makes sense."

Unfound in her world, I stood silent, serene,
unseen.
Immersed in the beauty of but a mere
interaction.
That hall, those eyes, and that smile
Shall remain a clandestine dream.
Counting stars till the day
That smile turns my way.

How many stories has she read? Nay,
How many has she lived?
On that shelf of memories, would there exist
An empty space for one more? For one more?
One ballad written just for us?

I'd pen each line with utmost care,
To surrender unto thee, a narrative full
Of laughter and joy, trust and hopes,
Of griefs, despairs and their repairs.

In that single moment, my planets
Rewrote their stars.
The future lent me a glimpse brief, into life.
A life which had her hand in mine.

And oh!
As the final bell rang, I knew,
Caught in her gaze, this
Flame would forever ignite.

Lucid Dreaming

Will these legs carry
Through the raging inferno?
I wonder if I shall be able to breathe.

Would this breath of mine
Rest upon the midday grass?
All the whilst I tumble, tumble
Into the pit of my sins.

Wouldn't this liver have the will
To help me quench one last drink?

Would it? Or, would it nay?
Nay! I say
I shall see way! Wayward walking
Upon the shore. Not bothered
By dreams of yore. Yores in which
My troubled mind did once whisper
To me a plan divine. Divine I say for
I know not if it were true. Not true,
Yet true nonetheless.

I ask. Nay, I speak again.
These legs shall carry me through the inferno.

Through the inferno to one Eden divine.
Where this breath of mine would
rest upon the midday grass.

Though I shall tumble, tumble
Through the pits of my sins.
I will find the warmest of summer,
inside my chilliest winters.
A flame which would warm
The ice upon my stars.

And as the sun would bid me "dieu
I'd take one last sip o' my brew.
Sing a hearty song in blue.
And fly my chariot across the moon.

Ode to the Pacific

Oh, vast and divine pacific,
Endless in thine expanse.
Thine waves whisper music,
To which the crustaceans dance.

Waves ebb and flow,
Tides come and go.
The majesty of waters clashing,
makes the eyes overflow.

Heaven. Oh dear heavens!
How I am mesmerized!
The way you are kissed,
By the golden fire of the sunshine.

Endless horizons!
Horizonless dreams!
A picture so very blue,
But with joy it gleams!

Carrying a million tales,
Eternal and ever profound.
Thine waters hold true horrors,

A life lost. Another found.

For the thousandth time

Behind those ebony eyes,
Lied a sullen tale.
Waiting to be told,
For the thousandth time.

Never was it comprehended,
Never was it liked.
Yet the soul persevered,
For the thousandth time.

He longed for company,
He despised the solitude,
He yearned for a soul,
Whom he could call his own.

The pain could not be erased
By mere drinks or smokes.
Yet he emptied a bottle
And puffed another toke.

Tossing and turning,
He laid awake all night
Snuffing out the whispers
That flooded his mind.

He was at his wits' end.
He couldn't endure anymore.
He shouted, "Let me be!"
For the thousandth time.

The morning after,
Was pretty much the same.
The sun was still shining.
The sun was still gay.

Not for him though.
It all had changed.
For, a pool of blood
Lay in his wake.

He had parted ways
From the cold and snowy land.
For he could not endure it,
For the thousandth time.

Darling and Honey

Someday when the sun freezes o'er,
And hell falls down the sky,
I will take an amble down the aisle,
With your arms wrapped in mine.

My darlin', O dear darling,
O' come and walk with me.
We'll walk past the meadows green
And through the valleys deep.

Hold this freckled hand as
We cross the mountains steep.
We'll lay down when the sun sets,
And I'll thank God you're with me.

O darlin', O dear darling
How do you love me so?
With tender hands you hold me
Till I cannot cry anymore.

O darlin', dear darling
Why did you leave with me?
Why did you trade the mink sheets
For this bed of earthy green?

Your mama said, "Dear daughter,
How could you treat me so?
If you leave with that rambler,
Consider these gates closed."

O' Mama, dear Mama,
You would not understand
The love that He and I share
Through happiness and despair.

O' Daddy, dear Daddy,
I've fallen hopelessly.
I cannot walk these pavements,
If my dreamer ain't with me.

My Angel, dear Angel,
My princess you'll always be.
I won't halt you from gambling,

Or gamboling with the breeze.

O' Darling, my dear Darling.
Why do you love me so?
I am but a lonely drifter,
You're as clean as the driven snow.

O' honey, my dear honey,
Why do you blame yourself?
I left the concrete jungles
For our love and this view scarce.